TRIBES of NATIVE AMERICA

Cherokee

edited by Marla Felkins Ryan
and Linda Schmittroth

BLACKBIRCH®
PRESS

THOMSON
━━━✶━━━
GALE

San Diego • Detroit • New York • San Francisco • Cleveland
New Haven, Conn. • Waterville, Maine • London • Munich

LIBRARY OF CONGRESS CATALOGING-IN-PUBLICATION DATA

Cherokee / Marla Felkins Ryan, book editor; Linda Schmittroth, book editor.
  v. cm. — (Tribes of Native America)
Includes bibliographical references and index.
Contents: Name — Origins and group affiliations — The Trail of Tears — From Indian territory to the State of Oklahoma — Religion — Language — Government — Economy — Daily life — Education — Customs.
  ISBN 1-56711-614-0 (hardback : alk. paper)
1. Cherokee Indians—History—Juvenile literature. 2. Cherokee Indians—Social life and customs—Juvenile literature. [1. Cherokee Indians. 2. Indians of North America.] I. Ryan, Marla Felkins. II. Schmittroth, Linda. III. Series.
E99.C5 C4144 2003
975.004'9755—dc21   2002007801

Table of Contents

CHEROKEE

Name

Cherokee (pronounced *CHAIR-uh-key*). The name comes from the Creek word *chelokee,* which means "people of a different speech." The Cherokee call themselves *Ani'-Yun'wiya',* which means "the real people" or "the principal people," or *Tsalagi,* which comes from a Choctaw word for "people living in a land of many caves."

NORTH AMERICA
Cherokee
Atlantic Ocean
Pacific Ocean
Gulf of Mexico

INDIANA
WEST VIRGINIA
VIRGINIA
KENTUCKY
NORTH CAROLINA
TENNESSEE ③ ②
SOUTH CAROLINA
① ARKANSAS
⑥
MISSISSIPPI ④ GEORGIA
ALABAMA
LOUISIANA ⑤

Cherokee
Contemporary Communities

1. United Keetoowah Band and Cherokee Nation of Oklahoma
2. Eastern Cherokee Tribe, North Carolina
3. Etowah Cherokee Nation, Tennessee
4. Echota Cherokee Tribe of Alabama

5. United Cherokee Tribe of Alabama
6. Georgia Tribe of Eastern Cherokees

Shaded area: Traditional Cherokee lands in the Appalachian Mountains in present-day North Carolina, South Carolina, Virginia, West Virginia, Kentucky, Tennessee, Georgia, and Alabama.

Where are the traditional Cherokee lands?

The Cherokee first lived in parts of what are now North Carolina, South Carolina, Virginia, West Virginia, Kentucky, Tennessee, Georgia, and Alabama. In the late 1990s, most Cherokee lived in northeastern Oklahoma, North Carolina, and Tennessee.

Col-lee, a Cherokee band chief, around 1834

The Cherokee have lived in North Carolina (pictured) for centuries.

What has happened to the population?

In 1674, there were about 50,000 Cherokee. From the mid-1600s to the 1730s, there were about 25,000. In a 1990 population count by the U.S. Bureau of the Census, 369,979 people said they were Cherokee. This made the tribe the largest in the United States.

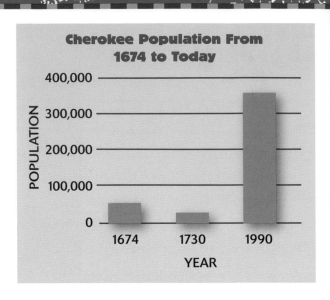

Cherokee Population From 1674 to Today

POPULATION

400,000
300,000
200,000
100,000
0

1674   1730   1990

YEAR

Origins and group ties

Many historians believe that the early ancestors of the Cherokee moved from what is now Mexico and Texas to the Great Lakes region. Then, 3,000 to 4,000 years ago, conflicts arose with the Iroquois and Delaware tribes. The Cherokee then moved to the southeastern part of the present-day United States. In the late 1990s, three main tribal groups and many other groups in at least 12 states claimed to have Cherokee origins.

A Cherokee man wears traditional war paint. The Cherokee are the largest tribe in the United States.

Before Europeans came in 1540, the Cherokee were farmers. They held 40,000 square miles of land. Over the years, the tribe lost many people to wars and diseases brought by the white settlers. The Cherokee, along with the Chickasaw, Creek, Choctaw, and Seminole, were known as the "Five Civilized Tribes." White people coined this term because these groups had ways that were similar to those of whites.

Europeans forced the Cherokee to move west from their original lands in North Carolina (pictured).

During the 19th century, the U.S. government forced many Cherokee to move far west of their homeland. This sad journey became known as the Trail of Tears. The Cherokee formed new schools and systems of law in Indian Territory. The government got rid of these, though, when the state of Oklahoma was created in 1907. This misfortune did not stop the Cherokee. At the end of the 20th century, they were the largest Indian group in the United States and had a high standard of living.

The Cherokee were forced to leave their homes in the Southeast, and resettle in Oklahoma, in the 1800s. This journey is know as the Trail of Tears.

• Timeline •

1540
The Cherokee are first visited by Europeans

1607
English colonists settle Jamestown, Virginia

1620
Mayflower lands at Plymouth, Massachusetts

1776
America declares independence from England

1821
Tribal leaders approve a method Sequoyah created to write the Cherokee language

1827
The Cherokee adopt a written constitution

1838
Cherokee leave their lands on a forced journey known as the Trail of Tears

1861
American Civil War begins

HISTORY

Trade with Europeans

The Cherokee people lived in towns in the river valleys of the southern Appalachian Mountains. Each town had its own chief, but there was no overall government. The Cherokee first met Europeans in 1540, when Spanish explorers passed through their lands. After that, the Cherokee had little contact with whites until the 1600s. Then, traders arrived. The tribe traded deerskins for goods such as metal tools, glass, cloth, and firearms. This trade changed Cherokee culture. The people no longer farmed and hunted

Cherokee men dressed in clothing like that worn in the 1700s.

The Cherokee traded deerskin with whites for tools and firearms.

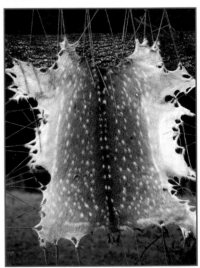

Some Native American tribes, including the Cherokee, fought during the French and Indian War. The Cherokee fought on the side of the British.

to survive. Instead, they bought and sold goods, and hunters, not priests, led Cherokee society.

The Cherokee fought on the side of the British in the French and Indian War (1755–1763) and the American Revolution (1775–1783). In the treaties that ended these wars, the Cherokee lost much of their land.

Divisions among the Cherokee

Between 1790 and 1817, some groups of Cherokee moved west as the number of white settlers grew. Most Cherokee people, however, stayed in their homeland. Then, a set of treaties between 1785 and 1806 caused the Cherokee to lose even more land.

Two groups formed within the Cherokee nation. One was called the Treaty Party. They thought the Cherokee should sell their lands in Georgia to the U.S. government and move west of the Mississippi River.

1865
Civil War ends

1869
Transcontinential Railroad is completed

1907
When the state of Oklahoma is formed, the United States ends the Cherokee tribal government and school system

1917–1918
WWI fought in Europe

1929
Stock market crash begins the Great Depression

1941
Bombing at Pearl Harbor forces United States into WWII

1945
WWII ends

1950s
Reservations no longer controlled by federal government

1984
The first modern-day meeting of the Eastern Band and the Cherokee Nation is held

A Cherokee woman on tribal land

Chief John Ross believed that the U.S. government would help the Cherokee keep their land.

The second group was the Ross Party, led by Principal Chief John Ross. This group thought the Cherokee should have talks with the government. They wanted to try to use the U.S. court system to keep what was left of their old lands.

The fight for the southeastern homelands

In the early 1820s, the Cherokee built a capital city in New Echota, Georgia. In 1827, they wrote a constitution that was like the U.S. Constitution. They wanted to set up their own government and keep their lands. The Georgia legislature, however, passed laws that put an end to the

Cherokee government. These laws also took Cherokee land for the state.

When Georgia tried to push the Cherokee off their lands, the Cherokee went to the U.S. Supreme Court. In 1832, the Supreme Court ruled that Georgia could not force the Cherokee from their land. This Cherokee victory lasted just a short time.

The dispute deepens

Even though most Cherokee were against it, the Treaty Party signed the Treaty of New Echota in 1835. The Treaty Party agreed to trade the tribe's land in the east for land in Indian Territory and for some money to help the Cherokee move.

Most Cherokee people were outraged that the treaty was signed. The Treaty Party was a small group that did not have the right to act for the whole tribe. Ross and 16,000 tribe members signed a petition to protest the treaty. Even so, the U.S. Senate passed it, and the tribe was told to move west within two years. Most of the Cherokee said they would not leave unless they were forced.

The Supreme Court, under Chief Justice John Marshall, ruled in favor of the Cherokee in 1832. This decision allowed the Cherokee to keep their land in Georgia.

Martin Van Buren was president of the United States when the Cherokee were forced to make the Trail of Tears journey.

The Trail of Tears

In 1838, the government began to force the Cherokee off their lands. Seven thousand government troops took the Cherokee from their homes. The Cherokee were held in disease-infested camps. Then they were made to travel about 800 miles to reach their new homeland.

The Indians set off on their journey with no food, supplies, or shelter. Many of them were on foot. At least 13,000 Cherokee began the march. Before it was over, one-quarter to one-third of them had died. The march later became known as the Trail of Tears.

In North Carolina, about 1,000 Cherokee were not removed because some state officials supported them. One man, William H. Thomas (called Wil-Usdi by the Cherokee), bought land in his own name for the Cherokee.

Three groups unite

As the Cherokee settled into their new home, a new group—sometimes called the National Party—tried to set up a new government. The National Party asked the two other Cherokee groups that already lived in Indian Territory—the Treaty Party and the Old Settlers—to take part. The Old Settlers resented the arrival of the newcomers, and the three Cherokee groups could not reach an agreement. Several years of violent conflict came to an end with a special day of unity in 1846. The Cherokee people agreed to make the best of their circumstances.

The Civil War divides Cherokee people

The U.S. Civil War (1861–1865) threatened to divide the tribe once again. John Ross at first hoped not to take sides. In time, he agreed to fight on the side of the South (the Confederacy). The Old Settlers and many others, however, joined the Northern (Union) army. Experts believe that 25 percent of all Cherokee people died in the Civil War.

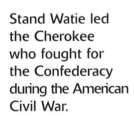

Stand Watie led the Cherokee who fought for the Confederacy during the American Civil War.

More broken promises

At the war's end, the U.S. government punished the Cherokee who had helped the South. It no longer honored treaties made with the Cherokee people. New treaties were signed in 1866 and 1868. They took large portions of Cherokee lands for railroads and for white settlements. These lands were also used to house other Indian tribes. The U.S.

government had promised the Cherokee people that no non-Indians would be allowed to settle in Indian Territory. But within 15 years, there were more whites than Indians in Indian Territory.

For years, the Cherokee had earned money by letting white ranchers use their land to graze cattle. The government stopped this practice in 1890, but did not say why. Many Cherokee had to sell their land to white settlers. The Cherokee then had worse luck. Dust storms forced many to leave their farms in Oklahoma in the 1930s.

In the 1970s, the U.S. government gave some federal money to Indian tribes. Since then, the Cherokee tribe in Oklahoma has become a national leader in education, health care, housing, and economic matters. The Cherokee Nation of Oklahoma adopted a new constitution in 1975 and elected its own officials. It began to govern itself once again.

Cherokee Nation of Oklahoma has its headquarters in Tahlequah.

Eastern Band of Cherokee Indians

As the Cherokee Nation adapted to its western home, those Cherokee who had stayed in North Carolina organized in the east. These people called themselves the Eastern

Band of Cherokee Indians. In 1924, the tribe reached an agreement with the U.S. government. This agreement made sure that the tribe would always own its eastern Cherokee lands.

In 1984, more than 30,000 people went to a two-day meeting. There, representatives of the Cherokee Nation of Oklahoma and the Eastern Band discussed their concerns. Such meetings are now held every two years.

A Cherokee man performs a traditional grass dance.

Religion

As far back as the 1600s, the Cherokee tribe had two sets of religious beliefs. Most believed that the world had been created by several "beings from above," who then abandoned it. The Sun took over and made plants, animals, and people. Then it watched over and preserved the Earth. The Cherokee who held these beliefs worshiped certain heavenly bodies, animals, and fire.

The other group of Cherokee believed in "three beings who were always together and of the same mind." The three beings created all things and were present everywhere. They had messengers who visited the world to take care of human affairs.

CHEROKEE WORDS

OH-see-yoh . . . "hello"
gog-GEE . . . . . . "summer"
wah-DOH . . . . . "thank you"
HOH-wah . . . . . "you're welcome"

A workbook shows the Cherokee alphabet.

A Cherokee war chief. War chiefs led during times of war while priests were leaders during peacetime.

Religion was part of the Cherokee people's daily life. Each year, festivals took place that were based on the seasons. Cherokee ways changed when Europeans came, and many Cherokee became Christians. Today, many Cherokee are part of Protestant Christian churches.

Government

In Cherokee tradition, each town had a chief who led in wartime and a priest who led in peacetime. Chiefs were guided by a town council made up of both men and women. In early times, the Cherokee did not have one chief who ruled over all. The entire group met only for ceremonies and wars. The post of principal chief was created in the 19th century to unify the nation.

The Eastern Band of Cherokee was formed in 1889. Its current government is made up of a principal chief, a vice-chief, and a 12-member tribal council. Council members are elected to two-year terms. The council deals with tribal issues, while another group runs the court system.

At the end of the 20th century, the Cherokee Nation of Oklahoma tribal government was made up of a 15-member elected tribal council. Its members served four-year terms and worked with a principal chief. The Cherokee Nation District Court took care of legal matters. An agreement made with the U.S. Congress in 1990 gave the tribe even more control over its own affairs.

Before they began to trade with whites, the Cherokee lived in homes like this one.

Economy

Before they met whites, the Cherokee farmed and hunted for a living. Women farmed, took care of the animals, and prepared the food. They made clothing, and cared for the house and children. Men hunted many types of animals.

CHEROKEE POPULATION: 1990 CENSUS

The Cherokee live in nine major groups throughout the United States. In 1990, the members of the various Cherokee tribes identified themselves to the U.S. Bureau of the Census this way:

Tribe	Population
Cherokee	352,680
Cherokee of Northeast Alabama	87
Cherokee of Southeast Alabama	196
Eastern Cherokee	5,968
Echota Cherokee	3,773
Etowah Cherokee	85
Northern Cherokee	285
United Keetoowah Band	145
Western Cherokee	5,811
Other Cherokee	5
Cherokee Shawnee	944
Total	369,979

Modern Cherokee dancers perform in Albany, Georgia.

A Cherokee man from one of the nine major groups within the Cherokee tribe

They also cleared fields for farming and built houses and canoes.

Before trade with Europeans, the Cherokee rarely tried to gain possessions or wealth. By the 1820s, however, many Cherokee had married whites and become landowners. They raised cotton and other crops on large farms and sold the crops for profit. When the Cherokee were removed, they lost most of their wealth.

The creation of the Great Smoky Mountains National Park in North Carolina helped to bring business to the Cherokee.

A Cherokee woman puts beads on a belt. Cherokee Nation Industries runs arts and crafts business for the tribe.

The creation of the Great Smoky Mountains National Park in the 1930s helped the Cherokee who lived in North Carolina. The park became the main industry at the Eastern Cherokee Reservation in North Carolina.

In the late 1990s, both the Cherokee Nation in Oklahoma and the Eastern Band of Cherokee in North Carolina ran bingo parlors to earn money. Cherokee Nation Industries, owned by the tribe, gave jobs to nearly 300 Oklahomans in its electronic parts factory. Most of these workers were tribe members. (The company also has other businesses, such as ranches, arts and crafts outlets, and a cabinet factory.) To try to broaden the economy, the Eastern Band of Cherokee invested in a mirror factory and a fish hatchery.

DAILY LIFE

Families

The Cherokee people were organized into seven clans (family groups). Family ties were based on the mother's side of the family. Usually, a woman lived with her husband, their children, her parents, her sisters, her sisters' children, and any unmarried brothers. Fathers felt close to their children but were not considered their blood relatives.

Cherokee family ties were based on the mother's side of the family.

Buildings

A Cherokee town had a council house, a town square, and 30 to 60 private homes. Around the town was a fence made of poles placed close together to protect the people from attack. The council house was a circle large enough to hold all 400 to 500 citizens for meetings and religious ceremonies. The town square was used for ceremonies, meetings, and social events.

To build the walls of the structures, small tree branches were woven between support posts and then plastered with clay and grass. Roofs were thatched with bark shingles. By the 19th century, the log cabin had become the most common type of Cherokee house.

Clothing

Deerskin was the most common material used to make clothing and moccasins. Clothing and shoes were sewn together with bone needles and animal tendons. Cherokee men wore breechcloths—garments with front and back flaps that hang from the waist. In cold weather, they added deerskin leggings, fringed shirts, and robes made of fur or feathers. Beneath their deerskin dresses, women wore long, fringed slips. They were woven or knitted from the wild hemp plant.

Each Cherokee town had a council house like the one pictured.

For festive occasions, the Cherokee wore accessories made from turkey or eagle feathers, dyed porcupine quills, or thread spun from bear or opossum hair. They also wore wristbands and armbands hung with horn and shell rattles. Shells, bones, and copper were used to make jewelry.

Men often decorated their bodies and faces with paint or tattoos. They wore earrings. To make their earlobes longer, they cut holes in them and put stones or bone into the holes.

It was common for the men of the tribe to pluck out all their facial hair.

Cherokee men grew a palm-sized section of hair on the crown of the head and then plucked out a two-inch-wide ring around it. The long top section was pulled through a decorated, two-inch-long piece of hollowed deer antler. Any loose ends around the topknot were decorated with a thick, colored paste. The hair below the plucked ring was cut short. Women used bear grease to make their hair glossy and decorated it with yellow or red dust. It was worn loose or tied in a high knot.

A Cherokee man wears face paint for a ceremonial dance. Men often painted their faces and wore elaborate accessories during festivals.

Food

Traditional Cherokee farmed, hunted, and gathered food. They grew beans, squash, melons, pumpkin, and other food crops. Wild nuts, roots, and fruits were gathered from the countryside. Food was dried for use in the winter months.

Women kept a pot of soup or stew hot at all times. A favorite food was a mixture of meat or fowl, corn, beans, and tomatoes.

Corn was the main Cherokee crop. One type was roasted, another was boiled, and a third was ground

Left: A woman grinds corn into cornmeal. Corn was the main crop of the Cherokee. Right: A favorite Cherokee meal included meat, corn, beans, and tomatoes.

into cornmeal. Ingredients such as dried beans and chestnuts were often added to cornmeal bread.

Fishing provided much food for the tribe. The Cherokee ate bear, turkey, rabbit, and other game. Deer was the most important source of animal food.

Education

From the time they were small, Cherokee children had to endure hunger and pain to learn bravery. They were also taught to respect the earth and other creatures, and to honor their elders. A boy learned male roles from his mother's brothers. They taught him how to hunt, make war, and perform ceremonies. A girl helped her mother and her mother's sisters so she could learn how to care for the house and children. She also learned to weave, garden, and make baskets.

Today, an education department oversees the schooling of Cherokee students of all ages. The modern-day Cherokee Nation offers job training and other programs for children, teens, and adults.

A Cherokee woman shows young girls how to weave baskets. It is a tradition for Cherokee girls to learn skills by helping their mothers and aunts.

Healing practices

The Cherokee believed that illness came into the world when animals became angry that humans intruded on their lands and killed them for food. Plants that were friendly to humans helped cure these animal-caused diseases. The root of white nettle, for instance, was used on open sores. A tea brewed from witch hazel bark was said to cure fevers. Tobacco juice was used to treat bee stings and snake bites.

The Cherokee believed that spiritual help could make the body heal. Priests served as doctors. They knew all the proper prayers and chants and the correct ways to apply medicines to the sick.

The Europeans brought new diseases that made the Indians sick. After a series of outbreaks killed half of the Cherokee people in the 18th century, many native people lost faith in their doctor-priests. They began to seek medical treatment from non-Indian doctors. Many traditional medicines are still in use, though.

The Indian Health Service now runs a hospital on the Eastern Cherokee Reservation. A number of hospitals, clinics, and local health programs serve the people of the Cherokee Nation.

Left: A Cherokee medicine man. The Cherokee believed they could be healed by a spiritual leader. Right: Witch hazel was used to make a tea that could cure fevers.

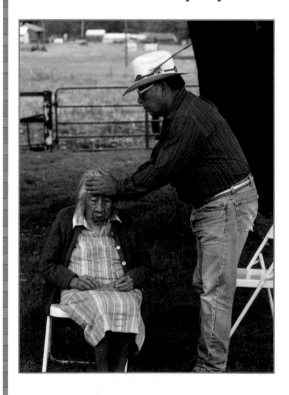

Arts

The Cherokee were known for the beauty of their carvings and basketry. They made tools, pipes, and canoes from materials such as stone and wood. For baskets, they used honeysuckle vine, cane, and wild hemp. They painted the finished baskets with dyes from plants and roots.

A stone pipe. The Cherokee were fine stone carvers.

Unto These Hills, a modern-day pageant that honors Cherokee history, is put on each year at the Eastern Cherokee Reservation in Cherokee, North Carolina. The Cherokee Nation of Oklahoma presents the drama *Trail of Tears* at an open-air theater in Tahlequah, Oklahoma.

Each year in Tahlequah, Oklahoma, the Cherokee present a play based on the Trail of Tears experience.

A Cherokee man wears a headdress made of painted wood and feathers for a ceremonial dance.

CUSTOMS

Festivals

Each year, the Cherokee held six major ceremonies. The main ceremony, the Green Corn Dance, took place at harvest time and celebrated harmony and renewal. At this time, all crimes of the past year (except murder) were forgiven.

Cherokee ceremonies are celebrated at "stomp grounds," sites for religious Stomp Dances. During Stomp Dances, people of all ages perform songs. They move to rhythms that create a sense of peacefulness.

A Cherokee dances at a powwow.

People of all ages participate in Cherokee ceremonies.

In the late 1990s, the annual Cherokee Fall Festival was held on the Eastern Cherokee Reservation. Cherokee Holiday, a weeklong celebration of Cherokee history and culture, takes place each year in Tahlequah, Oklahoma.

War and hunting rituals

Traditionally, dances were held before hunting trips. For example, the Buffalo Hunt Dance and Bear Dance, performed by both men and women, showed respect for the animals that would soon be killed.

Before Cherokee men went off to war, they prepared for several days. Warriors performed special songs and dances. In times of war, a Cherokee woman could take her husband's place in battle. Women warriors were known as War Women.

A Cherokee man and his grandson. Children learn about traditional ways at festivals.

Birth

Two days after birth, a baby was passed over a fire four times by a priest, who asked for blessings for the child. Four to seven days after the baby's birth, the priest took it to a creek or river, offered it to the Creator, and prayed for its long and healthy life. The priest then plunged the infant into the water seven times. An elder woman of the tribe then gave the child a name. This name reflected a trait of the infant or recalled an event that happened at

the time of the birth. The child might keep the name for life or take another name later, after some great achievement.

Funerals

Cherokee were buried soon after death. Female relatives cried and wailed the name of the departed one. Males put on old clothes and placed ashes on their heads. Relatives went through a seven-day mourning period, during which they ate little and could not show anger or good cheer. The dead person's belongings were either buried with the body or destroyed.

Widows were expected to mourn for several months and to neglect their personal grooming. Friends decided when a widow had grieved enough; then they washed her hair and dressed her in clean clothes.

Current tribal issues

Some native sources say that many whites falsely claim Cherokee ancestry. They do this so they can take advantage of government programs that help tribe members. Efforts are now made to make sure that such people are caught. At the same time, the Cherokee Nation of Oklahoma and the Eastern Band of Cherokee Indians work together. They want to make sure that their language and culture will stay alive for centuries to come.

Notable people

Sequoyah (c. 1770–1843) went by the English name George Guess. He had no formal education and spoke no English. Though he had a crippled leg, he fought in two European-led wars. Later, he saw whites who used written words. He decided to create a written language for the Cherokee people. Soon, thousands of Cherokee could read and write.

Wilma Mankiller (1945–) was elected principal chief of the Cherokee Nation of Oklahoma. She was the first woman to lead a major Indian tribe. She was re-elected twice.

Robert Latham Owen (1856–1947) was the second American Indian elected to the U.S. Senate. He served from 1907 to 1925, and was one of the first two senators from the state of Oklahoma.

Cherokee Wilma Mankiller was the first woman to be the chief of a major tribe.

For more information

Claro, Nicole. *The Cherokee Indians.* New York: Chelsea House Publishers, 1992.

Hoyt-Goldsmith, Diane. *Cherokee Summer.* New York: Holiday House, 1993.

Landau, Elaine. *The Cherokees.* New York: Franklin Watts, 1992.

Perdue, Theda. *The Cherokee.* New York: Chelsea House Publishers, 1989.

Sneve, Virginia Driving Hawk. *The Cherokees.* New York: Holiday House, 1996.

Official site of the Cherokee Nation   www.Cherokee.org

Glossary

Ancestors dead relatives

Clans family groups

Immune protected against

Origin where something came from or how it began

Reservation land set aside and given to Native Americans

Ritual something that is custom or done in a certain way

Sacred highly valued and important

Tradition a custom or an established pattern of behavior

Treaty agreement

Tribe a group of people who live together in a community

Index